The Online Community Blueprint:

A 9-Step Guide to Planning an Online Community for Your Customers, Members, or Partners

By Katie Bapple, Joshua Paul and Katie Oakes

Meet the Authors

Katie Bapple

Since 2009, Katie has been directing the growth and development of online communities. Prior to becoming the Director of Online Community Services at Socious, Katie worked for digital media publisher, Ziff Davis, and knowledge-sharing community provider, Toolbox.com, where she produced strategies for audience development, engagement, acquisition and ROI. Katie has helped numerous businesses, associations, and user groups to increase activity in their private online communities.

Joshua Paul

Joshua Paul is Senior Director of Strategy and Marketing at Socious, a leading provider of online community software to businesses, user groups, and associations. For the past 17 years, he has worked with digital strategies and technology product management to help companies grow through business model innovation, content marketing, and social media. Josh is a popular blogger and speaker on customer engagement, online communities, and social technology. Follow him on Twitter at @Joshua_D_Paul.

Katie Oakes

Katie Oakes is the lead editor of the Online Community Blog (blog.socious.com), where she publishes tips on online community software, strategy, and management.

Contents

Introduction

We begin this book with two truths:

TRUTH #1: Customer Engagement Fuels Growth

Customer engagement has a significant impact on your business. According to R "Ray" Wang, Principal Analyst and CEO at top advisory and research firm Constellation Research, "We see companies who have improved engagement increase cross-sell by 22%, drive up-sell revenue from 13% to 51%, and also increase order sizes from 5% to 85%."

Actively engaged customers are the lifeblood of business-to-business companies and membership organizations, like associations. These businesses rely on getting people to take specific actions, ranging from remaining a customer and using their products and services in a certain way to purchasing additional solutions and evangelizing the brand in the market.

When customers, prospective customers, and partners are more informed and engaged with your company, products, and resources available to them, these important audiences are more likely to respond to your campaigns, trust your messages, and convert on your calls-to-action.

A SOCIOUS PUBLICATION

TRUTH #2: Online Communities Keep More People Engaged Than Other Marketing Strategies

Building community has become the pinnacle of customer engagement. While you used to be able to keep your customers engaged with marketing campaigns or high-quality content alone, that is not enough to keep busy customers or members engaged.

While customer-to-company and customer-to-content communication is still important, customers who use social networks in their everyday lives and jobs expect to be able to engage with your entire community. Customer-to-community engagement strategies keep customers engaged by connecting them with your entire ecosystem of customers, partners, and employees.

Advice for Planning Your Online Community

Like any strategy that changes the nature of your relationship with your customers, creating an online customer community takes time, focus, and resources (primarily people). Bringing together your busy customers to share ideas, support each another, and produce invaluable product feedback does not happen overnight or even over the course of several weeks.

While creating a sustainable online community that provides value to both your target audience and your company is a long-term strategy, there are specific steps that you can take during the planning process that will eliminate rework, make you give your community members a compelling reason to participate, and increase activity from the start.

This book leverages Socious's 15 years of experience helping businesses, large user groups, and nonprofit membership organizations create thriving online communities for customers, members, and partners. You'll find proven tips for laying a solid foundation for your online community ranging from developing your strategy to defining policies that encourage participation to analyzing the right online community metrics for your community and business goals.

If you have any questions about applying the advice in this book or would like more information about Socious's online community software platform or services, visit www.socious.com.

A SOCIOUS PUBLICATION

Chapter 1

Choosing the Right Topic

So you want to create an online community.

That's great! Whether you're a company interested in providing a space for your customers to collaborate, an organization interested in uniting your members, or a niche interest group simply aiming to connect people with other like-minded individuals, your online community strategy can be a valuable part of achieving your goals.

However, planning, launching, and managing an online community can also be a lot of work and a substantial investment. That's why it's important to figure out exactly what type of online community you're creating from the beginning of the planning process. If you take the time to determine the right topic and target audience, you can avoid a common pitfall—creating a community with no purpose or audience.

Choosing the right topic might seem like an obvious step, but more goes into the decision-making process than meets the eye. What does choosing the right topic really mean? Why is it so important? And how can you make sure you do it well?

What Does It Mean to Choose the Right Topic for Your Online Community?

Though every online customer or member community follows its own unique path, they all start from a place of common interest. The formation of online communities happens when people join together around a common identifier. This can be anything such as a profession, hobby, activity, product use, or social factor.

You have a lot of leeway in determining this one specific item that unites all the members of your online community (or sub-community within the broader online community). If you are trying to position your organization at the center of your market, you might create a community based around a specific industry, such as HR, IT, or health care professionals (many associations take this route). Or, you could start a community geared toward a certain hobby or interest, such as jazz musicians or mountain bikers. The possibilities are truly endless.

Then of course, there are the online customer communities that center on a specific brand or product. Large companies with devoted consumers such as Starbucks, VMware, and Apple are well-known for their big online communities where people go and talk about the products because they feel so connected to the brand.

Regardless of the common identifier you choose to be the topic of your community, it helps if it's something people feel passionate about. However, this interest doesn't have to be their life's work. Your online community could focus on helping community members perform better in their jobs or advance in their industry. Often these are not a labor of love, but still something that people deeply care about.

Once you zero in on your topic, you may also want to combine it with a certain geographic area to increase the niche appeal. From there, your community might grow to have different layers of sub-communities for other interests or products that fit under your main umbrella topic.

Why is Choosing the Right Topic for Your Online Community So Important?

Again, choosing the right topic might seem like a no-brainer, but getting this step wrong can have disastrous consequences for your community down the line. The right topic can mean the difference between launching a successful, thriving online community and finally throwing in the towel on a community that just doesn't work.

Are There Enough People to Support Your Community?

The wrong topic might mean there isn't a wide enough audience to support the level of engagement your online community requires. While you want a community that speaks to a specific interest and area, you also want to make sure that the audience you're targeting is large enough to warrant the creation of this type of online social space.

Beware of Competition for Your Target Audience

Choosing the wrong topic could also mean you end up in competition with several other similar online communities and you aren't prepared to battle for your share of the audience.

If there are already several communities for your audience and they're doing well, it will be even more difficult to carve out your place in the market. Competing with pre-established online communities means you aren't just asking people to engage in your social network, you're asking them to choose to spend their valuable time in your community over another community where they are already comfortable.

Doing a little research in advance can help you choose a topic for your online community that sets you up for long-term success. Acknowledging the engagement potential of your prospective audience is the first step in ensuring you're creating a community that will be worth your time and investment.

How to Choose the Right Topic for Your Online Community

So, how do you know if you're choosing the right topic? While you'll have to rely on some degree of instinct and industry knowledge, there are a few questions you can ask yourself to help determine the strength of your topic.

Is There Already a Community for this Topic Online?

The answer to this question can help you assess your competition and determine if your community will be filling a void. However, even if the answer is yes, that doesn't necessarily mean your online community strategy is a no-go.

If There Isn't a Community for this Topic Already ... Why Not?

If your answer to the first question is no, take a minute to wonder why. Is it simply because no one has taken the time to create and manage a community? Is it because your online community topic is either too specific or too broad?

What is Unique about my Topic?

This question is especially useful if your answer to the first question was yes. For instance, there might already be an online community for avid knitters, but there might not be a community unique to people who knit and live in New York City.

What Makes my Topic a Community?

Once you pass all the other questions, it's time to think logically about how the members of your online community will actually function as a community. What bonds them together? How does that bond benefit from having an online community?

A good rule of thumb is to make sure your topic follows this simple and flexible formula:

Topic = Person who does X in Y

With this formula, X represents the common interest (whether it's an activity, hobby, profession, subculture, or product), and Y represents a geographical location, company, industry or cultural affiliation. Once you fill in the formula, you should be able to clearly define what your topic is, what makes it unique, and what makes it a community.

Takeaway

More often than not, a topic idea is the driving force behind the decision to launch an online customer or member community. While this is an incredibly logical place to start, don't move on from this step until you can confirm you've chosen the **right** topic. Take the time to consider other communities already in existence and how your new community will offer something unique to your target audience.

Chapter 2

Determining If Your Target Audience Will Engage

Once you decide on the perfect topic for your new online customer or member community, it can be tempting to hit the ground running with your launch plans.

However, before you get too far along, it's important to figure out your total feasible market size. By taking the time to assess your target audience's level of interest, you can determine whether an online community is the type of engagement platform your target audience is likely to participate in.

The Importance of Assessing Interest in Your Online Community

One of the earliest and most costly mistakes an online community manager can make in the planning stages is to assume people will be interested in what the online community has to offer. Even if you've taken the time to establish a well-defined topic and checked out any potential competing communities, it's impossible to know how your target audience will react to your online community without conducting marketing research.

Now, if the prospect of doing marketing research fills you with dread, don't worry—you aren't alone. Gathering data from your target community members and validating your ideas can be difficult to do, but the information you'll discover can be invaluable to the design and value proposition of your online customer or member community.

There are a lot of unknowns to launching an online community. This is the reason that online community strategies often stall before they get the green light from senior management. Basic market research can help answer some of the more daunting questions to better set you up for success.

Most importantly, proper research can give you the confidence that you have a target audience with a vested interest in your community platform from the very beginning.

In order to assess the interest level of your target audience before you launch your online community, follow **these five steps.**

Five Steps to Determine if Your Target Audience Will Engage With Your Online Community

Step #1: Figure Out Who You're Looking For

Before you begin surveying the market, you need to know exactly who your target audience is and where you can find them. Theoretically, you can probably sum up your target audience in one or two sentences, but finding them in the real world can be a bit trickier.

If you're a company creating a customer community, you have the added advantage of knowing your consumer base and can likely rely on brand affinity to get the feedback you need. Or, if you're an association creating a private member community, you can use your distribution list and existing member database to gauge interest.

Since these groups of people have already bought into your solutions or shown interest in your organization, seeking them out for feedback shouldn't be too much of a challenge.

However, surveying your target audience becomes a little more challenging when you're reaching out to people blindly. That's where step two comes into play.

Step #2: Use Other Social Spaces to Connect

Whether online or offline, you can generally find your target audience congregating in other social spaces if you know where to look.

- **LinkedIn**: LinkedIn has numerous very targeted and topically specific groups that would be a great place to start.
- **Twitter**: You can find people on Twitter using hashtags or keywords.
- **In-Person Networking**: There might be local groups in your area that are meeting offline and could be a good source.

By making it a goal to connect with five new people each week, you'll build up a strong contact base in no time.

Step #3: Communicate the Benefits

Your target community members are busy and have an array of online destinations competing for their attention. As you begin your research, make sure you take the time to tell your participants how your new online community benefits them.

They need to have a full understanding of your purpose and value in order to give you the type of honest feedback you need to make the best decisions for your online community strategy.

Take the time to explain why your online community would be worth their time and how they would participate so they can give you a clear and accurate assessment of their interest.

Step #4: Ask the Right Questions

Think carefully about what types of questions will help you assess the engagement potential of your member base. Aim to cover three types of questions: 1) interest level, 2) specific interests, and 3) specific activities. For example:

1. As someone interested in _____, would you join an online community where you could connect and interact with other individuals interested in _____?
2. What specific _____-related topics interest you the most?
3. In which activities would you be most likely to participate? Then list:
   - Connecting to other people interested in _____
   - Participating in conversations on _____
   - Writing or reading a blog
   - Online events such as webinars
   - Contributing to a wiki

These basic questions can help you zero in on both the exact interest level of your target audience and the specific topics and formats your online customer or member community should focus on.

Step #5: Be Personable

Reaching out to people you don't know to give you feedback on an idea they may not be familiar with isn't easy. Maintaining an open and personable rapport is essential to not only completing the research, but also hopefully convincing these members of your target audience to become members of your new online community.

Remember, a very small number of members can drive an overwhelming volume of community activity, so never discount the value of relationship building in these early stages.

Takeaway

Your online customer or member community deserves every chance to succeed. Set your platform up for success by pumping the breaks on your launch momentum and taking the time to assess your target market's interest level.

By conducting proper and detailed market research, you can get the scoop directly from your target audience without falling victim to the dangers (and resulting re-work) of faulty assumptions.

A SOCIOUS PUBLICATION

Chapter 3

Selecting an Online Community Platform

Choosing the best online community software platform for your organization can be overwhelming and confusing.

There are lots of great options out there; however, none are going to be a perfect fit. Narrowing down the advantages and disadvantages of each viable online community platform can be a serious undertaking—especially if you don't know exactly what you're looking for.

The online community software platform you choose directly affects the engagement experience of your customers or members. A frustrating or negative customer experience could impact your ability to retain community members and cause problems for the overall health of your online community. For instance:

- If they visit your community and can't figure out how to participate, or don't think the format is intuitive, they aren't likely to stick around.
- Customers or members are expecting your online community to live up to the experience they were seeking and a bad first impression could easily deter them from returning.

Picking the right platform is a decision that deserves careful consideration and targeted research.

Luckily, asking the right questions when you interview potential social software vendors can help you gather the data you need to make the right choice for your organization.

Here are some of our best tips to get the process started and help you find the best platform for your strategy.

How to Choose the Right Online Community Software Platform for Your Organization and Strategy

Give Yourself Plenty of Options

Even if a trusted colleague recommended a software platform or you have prior experience with a certain vendor, make sure you still take the time to research your options.

There's no harm in interviewing several choices to make sure you understand the features and support options are out there. Limiting your search creates the risk of implementing an incomplete solution and launching features that don't fit your goals.

Consider the Feedback from Your Market Research

Hopefully, you've already taken the time to survey your target audience to figure out exactly which features they're likely to use in an online community experience.

Considering this feedback as you narrow your platform search you can maximize participation once the community platform is live. For instance, if market research showed that your audience was most interested in a Q&A area or email-based discussion, make sure you select an online community software provider that offers that feature in some form.

Think About Your Specific Vision

No two communities are alike, so you want to make sure you find an online community software platform that speaks to your vision for your organization's particular online community.

Make sure you clearly communicate the environment and engagement opportunities that you want to create for your customers or members so the community software vendors you interview can detail how their platform addresses those priorities.

For example, say your ideal private online community is highly focused on collaboration. You want the capabilities for people to work together in groups, discuss problems, and connect through your community.

In that case, you know your platform needs a great discussion forum and group features, so you have a space to bring to fruition those opportunities for your customers or members. Identifying your priorities can help you narrow down your choices and select a community platform that aligns with your vision.

Be Mindful of Which Features Will Actually Get Used

It's easy to be drawn in by promise of innovative new features (every provider has them), but think carefully about which features will actually be utilized within your online community.

What Makes Sense for Your Audience, Organization and Strategy?

While it's important to have enough features to keep your community members engaged and give them reasons to keep coming back and participating, you also don't want to overwhelm your community with too many options. Offering a host of different social features that go unused can make your online community feel cluttered and disorganized, which could ultimately decrease your engagement in other areas.

Consider the objectives of both your audience and your company. If a feature doesn't address the objectives of at least one of those stakeholder groups, then it probably isn't something your community needs.

Remember, just because a software platform offers certain features doesn't mean you need to pursue it as part of your online community plan. While that might not necessarily mean you shouldn't pursue a relationship with that software platform provider, you also shouldn't allow the allure of less relevant features to sway your decision.

Ask About Updates

One important distinguishing feature of software platforms that organizations often forget to consider is the frequency of updates. If they haven't done more than two major releases in the last year, then you might want to think twice about selecting them for your online community.

A low frequency of updates might mean that functionality issues aren't typically addressed very quickly, which could have a big impact on your brand and the health of your online community.

Your members are also likely to become disenchanted with your community if it can't adapt to their needs over time. Frequent updates are a sign of consistent progress and a customer-centric company—two qualities you should look for in an online community software platform.

When interviewing potential vendors, right off the bat ask them how many updates have been made to their online community product within the last 12 months. The answer will tell you whether it's worth further discussing their platform or whether it's time to move on to the next option.

Takeaway

In the grand scheme of how many decisions you'll be making while launching your online community, your choice of software platform might seem fairly small. However, the wrong fit can have disastrous consequences for your engagement strategy and growth potential of your community. By asking the right questions and considering all your options, you can find an online community platform that serves your community, company, and goals

Chapter 4

Structuring Your Community to Optimize Participation

One of the most important decisions you'll make in the early stages of planning your organization's private online community is the structure of your interactive spaces.

While this initially might seem like a simple decision, the structure and design of your online community can significantly influence how and to what degree your members choose to engage. By being more intentional with your choices, you can ensure you're creating a platform in which your target audience will find it easy to participate.

Before getting into the how different online community structure choices can affect participation level, let's break down some of the basic options.

Structuring Your Private Online Community: The Basic Choices

Topically Specific

Since you've already determined the common identifier that unites your private online community, you may have also identified a few common sub-topics that could easily function as sub-communities under the umbrella of your main community.

Some examples of common sub-topics are geographic locations, specific products, or various interest groups. From there, you can decide which sub-communities need individual forums, file libraries, and events.

Role Specific

Or, if you're building a private online member community for an association, you may choose to structure your online community around the specific people who need access to various engagement opportunities.

For instance, you could break your community down into sub-communities—one for chapter members and one for board members. Then decide which features are needed for the members of sub-communities to perform their necessary duties.

Without Specificity

Lastly, it's entirely probable that you'll determine your community actually doesn't have many logical sub-communities and group, allowing one main space to be sufficient. Don't be alarmed if this is the case; sub-communities shouldn't be a structural choice that feels forced.

Now, let's discuss a few things to keep in mind when making structural decisions in your online community platform.

How to Structure Your Private Online Community

Keep Your Audience in Mind

Yes, you've already done your research to determine who your audience is, what they want, and if they'll engage with your new private online community. But that doesn't mean that the work of researching your audience is over. In fact, now that your online community is getting ready to launch, it's really only just beginning.

Keep your audience in mind during every single structural decision you make. Go back to that initial feedback your research provided and listen to the voice of the majority. By making sure that each feature you choose and sub-community you develop has the necessary interest level behind it, you can set your online community up to flourish from the beginning.

Build From The Bottom Up

In the beginning of planning any private social network, it's easy to get caught up in big dreams and plans for what your online community will eventually become.

However, in the planning stage, it's much more important to plan for the density you expect to have than the density you want. You can always grow and expand the space as engagement increases, but building from the bottom up (as opposed to the top down) will help allow that growth to happen organically.

Don't Overbuild

Even if you find yourself barely able to keep up with the flow of ideas and inspiration surrounding the design of your online community, avoid the impulse to overbuild.

If you create too many separate areas for participation too early in the process, your online community is more likely to end up with a lot of empty space. Instead, begin with a small number of areas for members to contribute to increase the social density (i.e. concentration of participation) in each space.

Here's the problem with empty space: your members won't feel motivated to engage if the participation in your community is already stretched too thin. When they see a forum that hasn't seen another response in months, they won't want to ask a question because they'll assume they won't get an answer. An excess of inactive spaces will only cause your members to ask themselves, "Why should I bother?"

Think Intuitively

The user experience of your private online community is hugely important to convincing your new members to return and continue participating.

As you're determining what kind of structure works best for your purposes, take the time to consider the humanness of your navigation.

- Will new members be able to easily determine their options for participation?
- Does the internal organization of your community have the potential to cause any confusion?

Put yourself in your future members' shoes so you can create a space that will elicit minimal frustration among your community members.

Here's an example of how to build out intuitive navigation for your community and sub-communities:

Community topic
- Sub-community topic
- Related discussion forums
- Related blogs
- Related wiki
- Related events
- Related document uploads

However, that's not to say that every sub-community needs every feature. Which brings us to the final tip . . .

Consider Features Carefully

Let's say you've decided to divide your private online community into a few different sub-communities that you feel strongly will be supported by your expected level of engagement. Next, it's time to consider what features, content, and engagement opportunities you'll make available within each sub-community.

Just like you don't want to overbuild your community as a whole, you also don't want to overbuild your sub-communities. If the topic of a certain sub-community doesn't support certain features, you shouldn't feel obligated to include them.

For example, not every sub-community needs a corresponding wiki or its own blog. Choose features your target audience has indicated interest in.

Takeaway

How you structure your organization's new private social network can have a make-or-break effect on how your members engage.

Being overly ambitious (or "overbuilding") with the structural decisions you make could result in a low participation density that creates too many empty spaces. People tend to find empty spaces and discussions without responses disenchanting, structure your online community for the level of engagement you currently have. The option to expand will always be there.

Chapter 5

Creating a Content Calendar for Your Online Community

When your private online community is just getting off the ground, there won't be much there. As more people join and participate in the community, the engagement opportunities for members will grow over time. However, in order to establish a clear value proposition for joining and participating from the very beginning of your launch you need content—original, useful, exclusive content.

Your community manager should plan to have at least two weeks of content present in every area of the community prior to launching and a plan for inputting consistent content going forward.

Just in case you think all online communities are not created equal, let's talk about why planning out your engaging content is so crucial for encouraging your members to participate.

Why is Creating a Content Calendar for Your Private Online Community Important?

Content Grabs Your Audience's Attention

When a new member arrives in your community, they need to instantly find something that grabs their interest and motivates them to participate. Otherwise, you risk turning them into lurkers for life or not returning to the community.

Using your online community content calendar to continuously publish high-value content in your community will help to remind your busy members to visit the online community. Eventually, they will come for the discussions and the content, but it is the content that initially attracts target community members, especially when there are so many online content channels competing for their attention.

Nobody Wants to Be the First to Participate

You can't expect your audience to visit your brand new community for the first time and begin participating. Often they need an example of how to interact. By filling in some of the empty space within your community before you invite members to join, you can model the behavior that you'd like members to take and mitigate the shy hesitation of newcomers.

In addition to having a few articles and comments ready to greet your initial online community blog visitors. You can also build out a few discussions in your forum spaces by asking some of your founding members or volunteers from your feedback council to get the ball rolling.

A content calendar facilitates the flow of ongoing value in your community and avoids dry spells that new online communities can experience.

Your Online Community Should Feel Like a Destination

If your target audience can receive the same information as a member from other channels they won't appreciate the value of being a regular online community member.

Making your online customer or member community your target audiences' one-stop-shop for important resources such as your file library and events calendar, it becomes a true destination for helpful advice and information about your organization.

A content calendar can help you stick to the routine of providing exclusive information that will keep your community members coming back. Despite how important consistently adding fresh content is to the success of a private online community, creating and maintaining a content calendar is a significant challenge for many community managers. So what's the source of this hang up? Why is sticking to a content calendar so hard?

The Two Reasons Organizations Resist Creating Content Calendars for Their Private Online Community

The Fear of Disingenuous Content

Yes, ideally your customers or members would organically create all of the discussions in your online community. However, the fear that user-generated content is disingenuous neglects to consider one of the primary purposes of your community: connecting your members to your organization. Having as many people as possible from your organization participating in your online community shows that your organization is invested in the community—which is an attractive quality to demonstrate to the people who are visiting your community and deciding how they want to engage.

The Belief That Members Will Create Their Own Content

Many organizations make the mistake of thinking once they provide an online community platform, their customers or members will just come and use it and build up the content and conversations on their own. Unfortunately, this isn't how online communities tend to work.

By making your content production process organized and consistent, you'll have a system in place to continuously show members why they should keep coming back to your community. This helps make it clear to your community members that your organization is not only invested in your online community, but that there will always be new value for members to absorb when they return to the community. Now that we've covered why creating a content calendar is important and what makes it such a challenge for organizations creating a private online community, let's get down to the specifics. How do you get started?

Four Tips for Building a Content Calendar for Your Private Online Community

Tip #1: Figure Out All of Your Features That Will Need Regularly Updated Content

Start by mapping out the content needs of your online community. This step helps you determine the amount of content you'll be creating on a weekly basis.

For instance, your calendar might start off with the content needed to supply the questions and answers in your forums. Next, you'll need to consider the blog articles you'll be posting and the comments you'll need to answer. You should also plan to regularly update your events calendar and file library.

Tip #2: Get a Little Perspective

While you'll probably want to break your content calendar down into a weekly to-do list, it's helpful to plan out at least a month or up to 90 days in advance. Don't plan beyond each quarter since you'll likely want to tweak your system, messaging, and tactics throughout the process based on the data and feedback you receive from your community members.

Your weekly perspective should show you the specific actions you need to do and how many times per week they require your attention. For instance, set a goal for how often you plan to respond to blog comments or forum questions. Ideally, that would be something you track every day to ensure that no more than 24 hours goes by without a response.

Tip #3: Delegate Responsibilities

Each task on your content calendar should be designated to a specific person so the delegation of responsibilities is clear. This helps to avoid any miscommunication and sets up a consistent routine for how to manage the different elements of content creation required to keep your online community running smoothly.

Tip #4: Be Open to Tweaks

Depending on how fast your community grows and how long it takes to grow, you might find that your calendar needs adjustments along the way. While sticking to your calendar is important, don't be so resistant to change that you continue following a procedure that your metrics show doesn't work. As long as you're making data-driven decisions, changes to your content calendar are simply part of the process.

Takeaway

The exclusive and helpful content within your private online community is a large part of the value proposition that motivates your members to join and participate. Stock your community with a week's worth of content prior to launching and consistently stick to a calendar that makes content creation just another part of your online community management routine.

Chapter 6

Acquiring Your First Prospective Members

One of the biggest concerns organizations tend to have when launching a private online community is whether their target audience will actually participate. How do you start from zero?

It's an understandable concern—who would want to make the upfront investment of creating a community only to see the space go unused? The good news is that, if you've properly vetted for your online community thus far, you're already off to a great start.

Remember when you were determining the viability of your online community by having conversations with your target audience? From this activity you gained two critical assets:

1. Personal, honest feedback, suggestions and insights
2. Rapport with highly engaged people

The insights gathered should provide invaluable information about how to create a solution that will directly address your audience's needs. How you illustrate that solution in your online community is your value proposition—the reason people will *want* to be part of the online community.

How to Find Your Online Community's Initial Members

The people who provided that data and insight when you assessed whether your target audience will engage in your community are your first prospective members. After all, they have laid out the building blocks of what will make your online community viable. In a way, they have also begun establishing a culture of active participation by agreeing to dedicate time to topically aligned conversations. They are the grassroots of your community. These people will help create qualitative value for others.

Getting buy-in won't be easy. These people aren't likely to step into the role without some motivation and encouragement on your part. It's imperative they understand the personal benefits for dedicating time to this new endeavor. Luckily, we have a few suggestions for engaging your first prospective members that can make launching your online community a more seamless process.

Four Steps for Engaging the Founding Members of Your Online Community

Step #1: Reach Out Directly

Capitalize on the relationships that you started to establish when you interviewed and/or surveyed members of your target audience. Since they've already had a hand in shaping the community's purpose, they will likely be more inclined to participate on a regular basis.

Identify a group of at least 60 contacts to count for attrition. Contact these individuals directly to let them know you'll be launching your online community soon. Be sure to note that their feedback had a significant impact on the community's final shape and purpose; as a result, you'd like to ask them to continue their integral role by being among an exclusive group of beta members.

Step #2: Do a Soft Launch

Before publicly launching your online community, give your first members time to interact with one another and provide feedback.

Make sure they understand how valuable their feedback will be during this time and be transparent about how you're using it. Then take their thoughts into account to work out the kinks before your community is made available to other members. Making these individuals feel valued and important will strengthen their loyalty to the community.

An important benefit to a soft launch is enabling these users to create genuine user-generated content before the community goes live.

Step #3: Develop Positive Behaviors

Once you have come to know this core group personally, offer special opportunities to promote their individual areas of expertise by asking them to author a blog article or lead a discussion.

Seed content and connect with key members, asking for their opinions and insights. When it comes time to launch the online community to a wider audience, use this content as part of the initial promotions by highlighting the conversations and article created by through this process.

Step #4: Offer Special Programs

Even if your initial members are incredibly passionate about the topic of your online community, it's important to constantly reinforce what's in it for them.

Continue to provide opportunities for these key members to feel important by developing special programs, such as feedback councils or recognition plans. Delegating power to key members will not only build loyalty, but help you scale community-building efforts over time.

Creating an active members base in new online communities takes a great deal of patience, dedication, and persistence. Don't rush the process and don't give up. Building relationships by reinforcing sentiments of belonging and importance is key for community adoption. Make direct member engagement a priority early on to drive participation and create a vibrant online community.

Chapter 7

Gaining Company-Wide Participation in Your Online Community

By now, we all know executive buy-in is important when creating an online customer or member community. Without it, community would hardly even be a discussion. However, getting your senior management on board is just a starting point. Writing a check, committing to a community platform, and getting marketing to send an email doesn't even scratch the surface. A foundation of unfaltering and abundant internal support is essential to building a successful community.

Having interdepartmental support within your organization provides the opportunity to create many wins, not only for the community team, but also many different business functions, as well as the audience itself. An "all hands on deck" attitude creates an unparalleled advocacy network for the community business case, and creates an internal paradigm that the community is as important of a fixture as marketing, sales or product.

Spend time championing your community to executives and colleagues; tie their participation back to goals in which they are personally accountable so they'll be excited about participating. Not only does their participation help create a more authentic community experience, but it allows them to step into the role of a community expert. They'll be able to field questions from members in a timely manner and aid in content creation. Your online community will be more likely to thrive as a result.

Not sure where to start the conversation? Here are three benefits of having an integrated community business strategy.

Establishing a group of internal participants scales community-building efforts.

Successful communities tend to grow more quickly when content creation is scaled across as many resources as possible. In most cases, your colleagues will be the subject matter experts of your online community's topical point of focus, making the responses and opinions they can offer invaluable. They are the gatekeepers of the information your audience needs. A simple request of each colleague (usually in a product role) for 2-3 responses to audience questions per day can take less than 15 minutes, but create a huge impact.

To keep the barrier to participate even lower, provide a daily list of questions needing answers in a collaborative location, such as Google Spreadsheets. Most online community platforms provide reporting that makes finding the appropriate content a breeze.

Quick, easy, reliable solutions makes for happy people who will continue to support and evangelize your organization's brand.

The presence of organizational involvement in online communities builds audience trust.

Clear employee involvement can help establish your organization's investment in the community—it shows that you aren't just trying to convince members to use the community; you're also using it yourselves. Furthermore, a public commitment to sharing knowledge illustrates that the experience people have with your brand is important, valued, and front of mind.

According to The Community Roundtable's 2014 State of the Community report, community's with internal executive-level participants saw 42% of members actively participating, versus 37% of members in communities without a clear executive presence. Online community members are extremely perceptive and will take note of a company's commitments towards audience satisfaction.

Creating opportunities for direct communication between audience and staff helps both parties achieve their goals faster and with greater purpose.

Depending on each colleague's position in your organization, explain how participating in the community helps achieve personal objectives.

For instance, if you want product managers to get in on the conversation, illustrate the opportunities for crowd-sourcing ideation. Letting real users tell them what items should be on the roadmap *and* what will likely make the biggest impact can highly improve overall user satisfaction. This not only makes your audience happy, but brings product managers closer to their goals in less time.

If you want members of the marketing team to help increase community awareness, show how member behaviors, dialogue, feedback and data empowers you to better understand the value propositions that make the audience you share tick. Guide marketers towards understanding how the information you have because of the community can increase their effectiveness to reach market segments, yielding greater reach through higher open and click-through rates.

If you want to encourage the CEO to publish a weekly blog post, speak to the corresponding benefits that someone in their position would find most encouraging, such as increased brand loyalty or higher renewal rates. End users appreciate transparency and opportunities to have their voice heard. By having the face of the company regularly address brand followers in way that communicates "we're in this together," the people who matter most to your organization will be more likely to see you through the tough times and rally by your side during the good.

Takeaway

Getting colleagues to take time out of their traditional roles to entertain new tasks is a huge challenge. It takes time, patience, dedication and a lot of ingenuity to make community a fully integrated business strategy. The key is to find ways that illustrate how the community can make jobs easier and goals more attainable.

Start with executive buy-in and ask for support. Prioritize departments with the most obvious gains for community participation by winning over team leaders. Follow-up by co-leading training sessions with the entire department.

Internal participation is one strategy in the overall community roadmap that is important to integrate starting from day one. However, it has a definitive place in all stages of the community lifecycle. The long-term success and needs of your online community will depend on it!

Chapter 8

Developing Moderation Guidelines

Thanks to the Internet, the world is incredibly interconnected; there are countless outlets for self-expression. The low barrier accessibility to digital communication and copywriting enables every individual to share the inherent strengths each of us possess via idealistic knowledge-sharing and the proliferation of divergent ideologies.

Unfortunately, the accessibility and anonymity of the Internet is often abused, showcasing the ill-willed and narrow-minded that aim to harrow attention from constructive human interaction.

Online communities are often victim to negative attention and antagonistic naysayers. By providing a platform for people to share their personal thoughts, you open the door for Internet trolls and spammers. In preparation, it's essential to have a plan for handling potential incidents by establishing a clear set of community guidelines.

An important step in creating a well-managed online community is to create governing documents that establish the online etiquette in your community. In most cases this entails two elements:

- A set of moderation guidelines
- A Terms of use

Both components have an important purpose in protecting the integrity of your online community and organization but serve essentially different purposes.

How to Create Moderation Guidelines for Your Online Community

So, what exactly are moderation guidelines? In general terms, moderation guidelines are a set of policies dictating what behaviors are or are not appropriate to exhibit in an online community.

While the exact content will vary depending on the subject matter of your particular community, the basic purpose is to:

- Set a standard for how members should interact.
- Define expectations for under what conditions interactions could—reasonably—be policed.

However, it's important to make sure your moderation guidelines work *for* your community and not *against* it. There's a delicate line that constitutes the difference between constructive and destructive discourse.

Stick to What's Absolutely Necessary

Members should genuinely feel like the online community is a place where they can express their own unique knowledge and opinions without being stifled. Moderation guidelines should not feel restricting.

Disagreement and controversy can be valuable to online communities due to their captivating nature—people invest time into topics they feel passionate about. Additionally, sense of inclusion within communities can flourish when community members have a reason to "band together" and "pick sides."

Therefore, if you operate under the knee-jerk reaction to delete every submission with suggestive or negative connotations, it will eventually backfire. Community members will feel discouraged from future participation if they only anticipate being silenced.

Undercompensate, Rather than Overcompensate

It's easy to get caught up chronically fearing worst case scenarios; the reality is that a very small number of people will act in ways that justify recourse. Because of this, it's better to undercompensate; you can always amend your moderation guideline as needed.

Start with a basic outline of appropriate community etiquette. A concise list of items to consider is:
- Unacceptable content and materials, such as those of an obscene, graphic or pornographic nature
- Inappropriate behaviors, such as hazing, bullying, defamation and intolerance
- Unacceptable community usage, such as commercial advertising or overt self-promotion
- Improper posting practices, such as thread hijacking, spamming, going off-topic and incorrect content placement
- How community members should handle complaints between one another

Keep It Brief

If you make your online community's moderation guidelines overwhelmingly lengthy, not even your most emphatic community member will feel inclined to read it. Not only do they not have the time, but they also don't want to feel like they're joining an online community that has a laundry list of restrictions. A general rule of thumb, try to stick to one page (or under 500 words).

Make It Easily Accessible

Moderation guidelines should always be housed in a static location within the online community. This can be as simple as placing a link in your site footer or a place on your community homepage.

On the page where the guidelines are posted, make it easy for members to locate the information they are looking for by providing anchor links for individual guidelines.

Community moderation policies exist to ensure the community is maintained as a safe, respectful and valuable destination for all members. By choosing to maintain an account in the online community, members agree to abide by these policies. Remove members who fail to benefit the community in a positive way and evolve community guidelines over time based on lessons learned.

While moderation guidelines help maintain a constructive community environment, Terms of Use address legal implications and copyright standards.

Chapter 9

Creating a Terms of Use for Your Community

Where online community moderation guidelines are your community's code of conduct, Terms of Use are its governing by laws.

Terms of Use describe an online community member's rights and responsibilities regarding the use of your online community. By using the community, they agree to enter a legally binding agreement on all the terms outlined in your Terms of Use.

However, even when certain terms are unstated, organization's reserve the right to change Terms of Use at any time. Also, governing copyright and intellectual property laws are always in play, even when not clearly expressed.

Therefore, a Terms of Use agreement not only holds the member accountable for proper online community usage, but protects the organization from reasonable liability.

Creating these terms can be overwhelming, so to get you started here are some basic elements to consider:

Personal Information

Since online communities usually have a personal networking component via online member profiles, it's important that individuals are held accountable for providing accurate information. Impersonation or sharing of account details are actions members should be held personally liable for; they should not be representative of negligent practices on behalf of the organization.

This might seem like a trivial matter, however, the nature of some communities can have a large impact on an individual's personal brand, livelihood and reputation within key networks. Users should know that your organization takes these matters seriously.

Use of Content

There is a wide variety of content shared within online communities. Instead of detailing proper usage for each type, relegating its purpose for personal use only should minimize a majority of misconduct, such as external sharing of member profile information, lead generation materials or private downloads.

Of course, selling, plagiarizing or circumventing security measures to steal content should be expressly forbidden.

As user-generated content can often be of a delicate nature, protecting organizations from disagreeable opinions expressed by others is paramount. Make reference to the Digital Millennium Copyright Act and the United States Copyright Act of 1976. The former expressly protects organizations from legal disputes resulting from third-party user-generated content.

Finally, it's important to express that once content is submitted to an online community, it becomes property of the community—not solely the member nor the organization, but all those with a vested interest. Why? When someone posts content in an online community, it doesn't singularly benefit the organization, nor the original poster; it benefits the entire online community.

However, to stick with legalese, by contributing content to an online community, members should realize that they grant a royalty-free and irrevocable right to the organization to publish, distribute or revise content (with exception to the disclosure of personal, private information).

Content Management

In online communities, it's important to acknowledge that content largely represents the collective work of individuals with varied backgrounds, viewpoints and ideologies. In choosing to use an online community, members should acknowledge that instances of extreme disagreement might arise. While these instances should not be viewed as a personal attack or cause contention between members, oftentimes grievances run wild. Terms of Use should reinforce the realities that the organization cannot be held liable for disputes resulting from content posted by other users. If this language alone doesn't silence legal threats, refer people to the Digital Millennium Copyright Act mentioned above.

Tie back to the private online community's moderation guidelines to reference appropriate behavior, but use the Terms of Use to explain that members are fully responsible for any negative actions resulting from their contributions. Organizations have no obligation to review content before it is submitted, but may edit or remove content if it is deemed to violate community moderation guidelines, to disobey laws or regulations, or to put into question the integrity of the online community or other members.

Disputes Between Users

This might sound like playing with fire, but it's a fact—organizations have no obligation to mediate or resolve disputes between community members. Community administrators reserve the right to act under their own discretion, whether it be taking an active role in a disagreement, modifying or deleting content, or removing the offending individuals' access to the community altogether.

Takeaway

This is by no means an exhaustive list of the items that can (and in some cases, should) be covered within an online community's Terms of Use. Specific language and terms will depend on the nature of the community itself. If your organization employs legal counsel, it's highly advised to work with them on this process.

With any luck, your online community with be a productive, active, and respectful space with members who truly want to get the most out of their participation and experience. However, in the event that you do have to deal with legal threats, inappropriate content and undesirable behaviors, you want to have the proper policies in place to aid in de-escalation. Setting the standards of behavior for your online community is an important aspect of online community management that shouldn't be overlooked. Lay the basic groundwork to protect the community and your organization; rest assured that you can always update and amend your policies as needed.

Chapter 10

Establishing Key Online Community Metrics Before You Launch

The launch of a private online community is often met with expectations from all sides—organizational leaders, community members, and the community management team. Each has their own definition of a "successful online community."

Your investors, board members, and upper-level management will want to see that your online customer or member community is a worthwhile financial investment. Your community members will want to see that your online community is a meaningful place to spend their time. Finally, your community management team will want to know where to focus their efforts and whether your current strategy is working.

So, how can you as a community manager show these results?

It is important to establish a process to collect and track specific online community metrics *before* your launch.

Tracking the right metrics leads to setting smarter goals, making better decisions, and ultimately gauging your online community's success. The data your online community yields is extremely valuable in terms of knowing what your target audience wants and how your organization can maximize its return.

But where do you start? Access the metrics.

Regardless of the online community software you're using, you should have an analytics dashboard or some type of reporting functionality that allows for easy tracking. Define not only which metrics to track, but the process to gather that data efficiently from the very beginning. Your online community software provider can guide you toward where each data point exists in their platform.

Taking this step before the launch will set you up for success. Tracking online community metrics after the fact is time-consuming, difficult, and often less accurate, so avoid the hassle.

The Four Types of Online Community Metrics You Can't Do Without

While the metrics you track will likely grow and change as your online community evolves, there are four types of data that you should be collecting right from the start.

Metric #1) Traffic

One of the biggest concerns we hear before companies launch an online customer community is, "Will people actually use it?" This is a question that keeps many stakeholders up at night. People who don't have experience managing online communities go directly to talking about website traffic. However, as a community manager, you should be measuring more than the number of people coming into your online community.

Break down your traffic metrics to include:

- Where are your page views coming from?
- Are your members logging and visiting multiple pages?
- Are they logging in and staying awhile?
- Are they logging in more than once?

Knowing where your traffic is coming from determines which marketing efforts are working and which you may need to revisit. For example, if you launch an email campaign and your site traffic doesn't really jump, is it because you subject line was faulty, the call to action was off, or maybe it's time to focus your efforts elsewhere.

You won't truly know without measuring your traffic metrics correctly.

Metric #2) Activities

Once you know the amount of traffic your online community is receiving, you can begin determining how people are participating. When we use the word "activity," we are talking about the actions community members take once they are on the site. Start tracking their activity with metrics that include:

- Where are they spending the most time?
- What forums are attracting the most activity?
- What types of blog posts are the most popular?

When you have a clear idea of how your members like to use your community, you can design a better experience for them based off the interests and tendencies. Tracking this metric tells you not only which topics your members want but also how they want to consume that content (i.e. videos, forums, etc.).

Metric #3) Members

Ideally, your online community would bring in new members every month, but simply tracking your accumulative member count doesn't tell the whole story. You need to know how many members are new each month and why that number is growing or declining over time. Set in place a process to monitor:

- How many members are leaving each month?
- Are new members are getting involved and taking action in the community?
- What types of members are leaving? For instance, if a member who has never taken the time to participate leaves your community, it

tells a much different story than if an active member decides to leave.

It would be impossible to track down every member that leaves your community. However, if you start to notice a dip in active members, it may be time to offer a poll or survey to check on the health of your online community. You want to be proactive instead of trying to make up a deficit later.

Metric #4) Subscriptions

Tracking the subscription rates for your blogs and forums helps you to analyze interest levels in those areas. If a particular blog in your community or discussion forum has a low adoption rate, it may mean that there isn't enough interest within your online community to justify the continuation of that engagement opportunity.

However, on the contrary, high subscription numbers can tell you what type of information and engagement garners the biggest response from your members. By knowing which content interests your readers, you can provide consistent value for your members that will keep them engaged.

Takeaway

These metrics are simply a starting point as you plan the launch of your online customer or member community. Every online community is unique.

Before launching your new private online community, it's important to establish the key metrics you'll be tracking and a process for collecting that information on a consistent basis.

The data you collect from your online community can help inform the community management decisions you make and demonstrate different areas of success to impatient stakeholders. Keeping these records from the very beginning of your community's lifecycle allows you to compare growth over time as you learn what works and what needs improvement.

Chapter 11

Getting the Most From Online Community Metrics

Seasoned community managers know that data-driven decision making is essential to growing and managing perpetually active online communities. According to The Community Roundtable's State of Community Management research, "best-in-class online communities are almost twice as likely to be able to measure their value to the organization."

While there is a lot that goes into managing a thriving online community, the same report notes that online community management teams that can report on their community's value to the company are tracking many more metrics than average online communities.

We have previously written about key online community engagement metrics and the importance of establishing a process for tracking the right social metrics during the online community planning process. However, what you do with that data is just as important to your ability to make data-driven community management decisions.

Once you have routinely compiled a plethora of meaningful data from your online community, it's time to analyze.

The following are three proven tips to getting the most out of your hard-earned online community analytics data.

Uncover Your Biggest Opportunities and Biggest Challenges

How you analyze and interpret the metrics you collect in your online community software platform determines how effectively you make data-driven decisions for your private online community.

The data you collect provides the roadmap for steering your community on a weekly, monthly, and quarterly basis. Your community platform's analytics provide an accurate representation of where your community is performing well and where it could do better.

Your data makes it easy to take an honest look at what is working and what isn't in your community. For instance, if there are groups that the active online community is avoiding, don't waste time building content for those areas of the community. If you notice that a lot of people are coming to your online community from social media, take that opportunity to increase the content you put there.

In contrast, when your online community metrics highlight that most community members are logging in, and looking at only one page, it is outlining your next challenge. Rather than wondering why activity has dropped off in your online community and potentially chasing the wrong solution for weeks or months, your data can point you to exactly where the problem is and which community members you need to re-engage.

Look at your online community analytics data as early-warning signs for both opportunities and challenges to structure your online community's evolution and adjust your community management processes.

Show the Metrics to the Right People

Once you have collected valuable data, it is important that you share your results with the right people. Share your data so that the right people are updated on the overall health of the online community.

Keeping key players inside your company informed about the growth of the online community can ignite additional organizational participation and funding. Company-wide participation is a foundational pillar in successful and sustainable online community. So, who qualifies as the right people?

It goes without saying that every member of your online community management team should be aware of those key metrics regularly. This team should also have a very clear understanding of what goes into the collection and recording of your metrics.

Beyond that, you should share your data with those in leadership roles overseeing the community strategy and other stakeholders. Don't be afraid to communicate the data as high up the chain of command in your organization as possible.

Your online community's performance data is crucial to communicating the value of your online community and how it increases over time, so sharing your numbers can help your senior management become more interested and invested over time.

Stay on Schedule

A common question we hear is, "how often do I need to record data from my online community?" The answer isn't simple and there isn't just one answer to this question.

Every online community has a unique set of goals, audiences, and tools that play a role in gathering the right metrics. Your business will need to assess all of these factors when you are putting analytics and reporting processes into places.

Each metric may have a unique schedule for collection. Some metrics might need to be updated weekly if you have certain goals that depend on the information they provide. Others may need to be reviewed once a month to really show the full picture of what's happening in your online community.

The key to success is staying true to the process that you create. Once you have a collection plan in place it is crucial to abide by that plan. You are most able to make decisions based on your online community data when it is collected regularly.

You are trying to build a complete picture of your online community. When you forget to collect here or there, your conclusions can be off significantly—causing rework, wasted time, and confusion.

Takeaway

While online community metrics give you actionable data to steer your online community and member interactions, it also provides the validation that your strategy's stakeholders will ask for sooner or later following your community's launch.

Accurately recording community data gives your organization the power to make smart, data-driven decisions and take calculated risks in your online community. The data you collect from your online community will inform the community management decisions you make and demonstrate different areas of success to impatient stakeholders.

Keeping these records from the very beginning of your community's lifecycle allows you to compare growth over time as you learn which tactics works and where you have opportunities to improve your online community.

Chapter 12

Soft Launching Your Online Community

After months of strategizing, planning and hard work, you're finally ready to launch your new online community. Your online community software vendor has completed the implementation process, your community layout is all set up, and you have a handful of active members ready to engage with newcomers.

You're ready and excited to watch your efforts begin to pay off. However, before you jump headfirst into your launch, there's one just step left to take: a soft launch.

Taking the extra time to do a soft launch of your online community allows you to confirm that every aspect of the community is going to make a positive first impression on your customer, members, or partners. Even the communities that are 100% sure that their online community is ready for launch uncover hidden issues with a soft launch.

Still not convinced? Here are six more reasons to make the case for soft launching for private online community platform.

Six Reasons to Soft Launch Your Online Customer or Member Community

Reason #1: Guarantee Your Platform is Bug-Free

It's difficult to know how your platform will resonate with your audience until you put it into action. A soft launch of your online community to a small group of members allows you to monitor how the platform works to see if the process is intuitive or if adjustments need to be made.

Reason #2: Determine If You Have Enough Content Already Created

The content in your online community will grow over time—but it's still important to make sure you have enough exclusive content ready before launching to keep your new members interested. However, figuring out exactly how much content you need can be a tricky process. A soft launch gives members the opportunity to test-drive those resources and see how your audience reacts. This will also allow you to gauge the engagement level of the community atmosphere and identify any topics or resources you need to create to fill in the gaps.

Reason #3: Observe Your Members' Reactions

When you invite a few founding members into your online community for a soft launch, one of the biggest advantages is getting feedback on their first impressions. This first impression data can often be the only time you get this type of feedback when it comes to new members. Thus, having the opportunity to practice and adjust your first impression is golden.

Gauge their initial sentiments on the feel, use, and features of the community and take their reservations into consideration before you open the doors to your entire target audience.

Reason #4: Uncover Issues Your Testing Can't

A soft launch can help reveal hiccups or inconsistencies that your own testing of your online community may not uncover. If you are as excited about implementing an online community strategy as most organizations that we work with are, chances are you are very close to the project. You have been immersed in the details and minutia of your online community for months. You know it like the back of your hand.

However, you aren't the target audience. It is always best to have an outside reviewer, such as a member of your target audience, take a look to catch things you did not as the creator. For instance, while you may have thought that your choice for organizing your community platform and the resources within was the best decision, a soft launch with real community members could reveal a better option. Small changes and tweaks can make a big difference to the user experience.

Reasons #5: Lower the Impact of Missteps and Adjustments

If there are small issues or changes that need to be addressed before your online community officially launches, a soft launch enables those changes to affect fewer people. It's the difference between 1,000 members seeing a mistake and only 50 members see it.

Reasons #6: Slow and Steady Membership

If you create a big fanfare around the official launch of your online community and invite your entire target audience in at once, you're going to see big numbers—at first. These numbers are likely to taper off significantly as you find your core audience.

While your community's membership growth may rebound over the next few months, the initial big numbers followed by a big plummet can be discouraging. Save yourself the heartbreak by introducing the community gradually to grow and build engagement over time.

How to Create a Soft Launch for Your Online Customer or Member Community

Creating an effective soft launch is easy with the steps below. Use this as a guide to get you started on the process. However, bear in mind that every community has unique goals, strategies and characteristics that should be taken into account throughout the process.

Start Small

In order for a soft launch of an online customer or member community to have the most value, it's best to keep the number of people you launch with small.

The approximate sample size depends on the expected size and interest of your online community. However, aim to find the sweet spot of having enough feedback, but still keeping the community experience inclusive.

Smaller communities (under 1,000 members) may have a soft launch of just 20 people, while a larger community (above 1,000) may have as many as 75.

Where should you prospect to find these users? Look to those founding members who helped provide early feedback and research when you were still in the planning stage of your online communities.

Perfect the New Member Welcome

In order to collect the most valuable feedback from your founding members you want diversity in user experiences.

Encourage users to explore as many different aspects of your online community as possible. Test out your onboarding strategies by suggesting very specific activities one at a time. Avoid overwhelming new community members with options or being too pushy. Gently nudge them to try different options within the community so you can get an accurate representation of how your target audience will engage.

Take Their Feedback Seriously

Soft launch participants should feel that their opinion is highly valued—they'll be more likely to be honest and take the experience seriously.

Reach out to them directly for their feedback through phone calls and personal emails. Make sure the questions you ask are specific so you can get a full understanding of what's working and what still needs to be tweaked.

Focusing on direct outreach with your founding members demonstrates that their role in the process is important, which helps to create a stronger sense of community and belonging that will carry over to the official launch.

Collect Data

Soft launching your online customer or member community is a great opportunity to perfect your data-collection methods. Test out processes and make sure you have a solid understanding of the social community metrics you'll be tracking. The soft launch data will obviously be substantially different than a busy month in your fully launched online community. However, it is valuable to have those numbers for comparison's sake down the road.

Takeaway

Launching an online community takes months of hard work and strategic planning. Don't fall short at the end and skip the crucial step of a soft launch. A soft launch gives your online community the chance to practice making a killer first impression on your entire target audience.

Simply testing the site within your online community management planning team is not enough. Engaging outside reviewers is key.

Don't miss the opportunity to gain valuable feedback from community members that will ensure your big online customer or member community launch is a major hit with your target audience.

Go Forth and Build Community

If you have never launched an online community before, it can be a daunting task. Developing a new, long-term component of your organization's strategy from scratch means you are in charge of the building blocks that will ultimately support or impact the investment's success. How the online community is positioned and put together from day one is critical. The key is to prepare, assess and strategize. With simple planning and a clear vision, a smooth and successful launch is easier than you ever anticipated.

Over the last few chapters, we have been chronicling the steps it takes to launch a successful private online community. To recap, we have created this to-do list to ensure you stay on the right track towards developing a thriving and successful online community.

Nine Steps to Successfully Prepare For the Launch of Your New Online Community

Step 1: Define a Topic

Communities are formed when people associate with one another around a common identifier. What will be the identifying topic that brings your community together? This can be a profession, hobby, activity, product, cause or social factor, just make sure the topic is unique to your community. If there isn't a vacancy in the market for your concept, you will struggle to grow a user base. Competing with pre-established online communities that cater to an identical audience is extremely difficult and will impede on member acquisition rates, as well as long-term retention.

Step 2: Assess Level of Interest

Speaking of member acquisition, before launching an online community, it's important to figure out your total feasible market size.

There are two questions to consider here:

- Are there enough people interested in your concept for the member-base to grow over time?
- Are these people already collaborating in other online communities?

Find out by doing a competitive analysis and reaching out to a segment of your target audience. If you don't already have access to topically aligned contacts, set a goal to connect with five new individuals each week via outlets like LinkedIn or Twitter.

Note that throughout this process it's important to reach out to target audience members at a personal level. The rapport you build with these individuals will become increasingly valuable to your community's long-term success. A very small number of members, especially in the first years, can drive an overwhelming volume of community activity.

When you are ready to begin having conversations with your target audience, be sure to assess their behavioral inclinations and social affinity for different collaboration opportunities (they will give you a head start on the next three steps we are going to cover). Also vet for the type of resources people will find most compelling and the triggers that will best solicit their participation.

Here are a few examples:

- As someone interested in _____, would you join an online community where you could connect and interact with other individuals interested in _____?

- What specific _____-related topics interest you the most?
- In which activities would you be most likely to participate?
- Connecting to other people interested in _____

Step 3: Select a Platform

If a majority of prospective audience members responded favorably to your online community concept, it's time to start evaluating vendors. Keep in mind the activities your audience expressed interest in so you can choose a product that will maximize participation. For example, if feedback showed that your audience is most interested in an area for Q&A, look for a vendor that makes this kind of participation as easy and intuitive as possible, such as email-based participation (also known as listservs) or file sharing.

When interviewing potential vendors, ask how many updates have been made to their online community product in the last 12 months. If they can't answer this question, or the number is small, move on. Members will become disenchanted with your community if it is unable to adapt to their needs over time.

Step 4: Create a Community Layout

By now, you should be acquainted with your target audience, their needs, and the capabilities of your online community platform of choice. As a next step, decide whether or not the common identifier your community is centered around has important sub-topics in which different sub-communities would help facilitate participation. For example, if you are starting an internal community for your organization (the common identifier), each department can be a sub-topic in which different sub-communities can be created.

However, be careful with this. If you create too many separate areas for participation too early on, you will have a lot of empty spaces. It is best to start with only a small number of areas for members to contribute so you will have a higher density of participants in each space. As specific sub-topics become more prevalent in member contributions, repeat the outreach process from step 2 and build sub-communities when there is dedicated buy-in.

Once you have defined the structure of your community and sub-communities consider what features each area will need. A community layout should easily fit into an intuitive navigation and include the following items (as applicable):

Community topic
- Sub-community topic
- Related discussion forums
- Related blogs
- Related wiki
- Related events
- Related file libraries

Step 5: Create a Content Calendar

Since all communities start at zero, it's important for the community manager to instantly establish engagement opportunities that illustrate a clear value proposition for joining and participating in a community. The community manager should plan to have at least one week's worth of content present in the community before launching, and at least one week of content planned for the week following.

Content calendars should include a mix of contribution types–discussion group questions, blog posts, etc.–that cover broad, general topics. A good volume of contributions to aim for would be 1-2 per day, per each staff member involved in managing the community.

In order to master the art of planning and creating compelling community content early, a content calendar is a key tool at all stages of private online community development.

Step 6: Establish a Group of Founding Members and Recruit Experts

Remember all the connections you made when surveying your target audience? Reach back out to those people to let them know that, based on their feedback, you are preparing to launch a brand new online community for people just like them! Invite these individuals to help shape the community by becoming a founding member and offer to highlight an initial contribution they have authored on a community landing page, or in the community's first email promotion. This group will be your first set of active members and help to establish strong peer-to-peer ties that build attachment.

Inside your company, recruit stakeholders to act as experts in the community. These individuals will ensure new questions coming from members will get helpful responses in a timely manner.

Successful communities grow much quicker when content creation is scaled across as many resources as possible, so continue to grow these two key groups!

Step 7: Create a Moderation Policy and Terms of Use

Unfortunately, some people come to online communities to attract the wrong kind of attention. Be prepared in advance by establishing a clear set of community guidelines.

A moderation policy should be seen as a guide to online etiquette and detail what is and what is not okay to post in the community. Include a link to these guidelines in the community so members can easily reference this document.

A detailed Terms of Use is equally as important, as it will protect the company from any legal liability based on the contents of user-generated content. The Terms of Use should be seen as a governing document for the community by acknowledging all implications of a member's use of the online community and how it relates to the rights of the company.

Step 8: Establish Reporting to Track Key Community Metrics

Before your community goes live, ensure that you will have access to reporting on community activity, traffic, subscription and member acquisition data. You will need to follow these numbers closely to gauge where to focus your efforts, what is working and what is not. Make sure you have a spreadsheet or report that will track the full history of each data point over time.

It's also recommended to set goals for the community's first six months. These goals should be easily measurable, and attainable but aggressive.

Step 9: Do a Soft Launch

You're finally ready to launch your new online community! Your vendor has completed the implementation process, your community layout is all set up and you have a handful of active members ready to engage with newcomers. However, before announcing the community to the masses, spend some time ensuring the community is ready to make a positive first impression.

Ask yourself these questions:

- Does the platform appear to be bug-free and intuitive? If not, what adjustments can I make?
- Has enough content been created to provide an engaging atmosphere for new members? If not, what topics are missing and what resources can I use to fill the gaps?
- What are the initial sentiments of the founding members on the feel, use and features of the online community? If there are reservations, what tweaks can be made to better address the target audience?

If you have these three key concerns figured out, congratulations! You can now move forward in managing and growing your own online community. Start by putting the items you learned and prepared throughout the launch process into action, such as direct member engagement, process-driven content creation and ongoing data analysis. Over time, you will see these simple building blocks create a strong foundation for your online community.

Happy community building!